DESIRES DREAMS AND THOUGHTS IN BETWEEN

This edition 2013
DoctorZed Publishing
10 Vista Ave, Skye South Australia 5072
www.doctorzed.com

Cover image
© Marilyna | Dreamstime.com

Cataloguing-in-Publication information can be obtained from the National Library of Australia

ISBN-13: 978-0-9875975-3-3 (sc)
ISBN - 13: 978-0-9875975-2-6 (e)

Layout design by Anna Dimasi

Printed in Australia, UK and USA

Acknowledgment

Life's journey's many pathways have fed me through the years
with laughter love and fun times, uncertainties and fears;
my family and friends have a place deep in my heart
and together form the base of the words which I impart.

Experience brings wisdom, knowledge gained, lessons learned-
these phases through my life are where empathy is earned.
Grateful for each moment that has helped me understand
that positives and happiness travel hand in hand.

Beauty is beneath the skin, simple things bring pleasure
and loving life is choice, which I consider treasure.
Many thanks and gratitude to every shining soul
who has deeply touched my heart and helped me with my goal.

❖

ᴅᴇᴅɪᴄᴀᴛɪᴏɴ ᴘᴏᴇᴍ

To my precious family,
you all mean the world to me;
Son Mat and daughter Riggy,
Grandson Ry and babes to be,
I dedicate these poems
each created from my heart,
so in many years to come
when it's my time to depart,
you'll have a little token
of the thoughts inside my soul,
to add to your endeavours
as you each pursue your goal.

I love you all

CONTENTS

desires

life

infinite

DESIRES DREAMS AND THOUGHTS IN BETWEEN

Desires, dreams and thoughts in between
are the assets enriching our minds,
leading us forth with positive threads
as life's journey forever unwinds.

❉

Entirely ours to shape and design,
to place on hold or to realign,
creatively customized with style,
moulding our magic that feels worthwhile.

❉

Infinite inklings may filter through,
surveying the scopes of thoughts anew,
no limitations lingering round
here, where horizons of hope are found.

❉

Desires, dreams and thoughts in between
are the jewels in our own treasure chest,
leading us forth with positive threads
as we're striving through life at our best.

friends

precious

2

*T*HOSE *F*RIENDS

*T*hose friends who find our inner selves
and sense our highs and lows
are treasures truly valuable
as budding bond-ship grows.

❈

*W*hen sunshine smiles through our front door
and lines our lives with glee,
our loyal friends are cheering too,
delighted as can be.

❈

*S*hould sadness strike a different note,
true friends will lend an ear,
sharing a shoulder blessed with warmth,
tending a trickling tear.

❈

A gracious gift is a real friend,
great wealth beyond compare,
more precious than a gleaming gem
and not found everywhere.

❈

*I*ndeed we're honoured when such friends
merge into life's long ride-
let's cherish and respect this love
that warms our hearts inside.

GIFTS OF GIGGLES

Gifts of giggles and gregarious smiles
foster fresh feelings that flow on for miles,
boosting the body with bubbles of glee
and wafting like waves that roll with the sea.

❃

Join in the laughter, let loose and embrace
expressions of awe employed on your face,
with eyes of excitement that beam so bright
they light up the sky as stars in the night.

❃

Cherish the charm from those giggles and grins
and share them around so everyone wins,
by fuelling our hearts with happiness hues
that colour tomorrow how'er we choose.

embrace

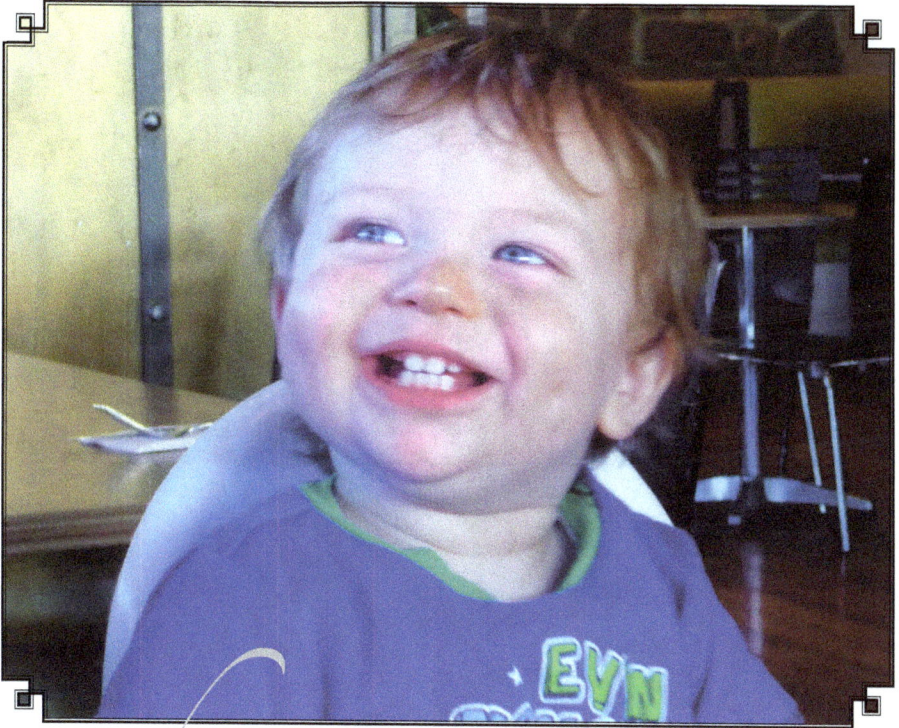

happiness

enriching

amazing

memories

Triumphant are Treasures

Triumphant are the treasures trickling into our day,
moments moulding memories that never go astray,
invested by the beauty that comes before our eyes,
most often laced with love and a welcoming surprise.

❀

Enriching us with value we store inside the heart,
are the simplest things in life that truly form a part
of our happiness within, which brightens up our view
by fuelling our fulfilment in everything we do.

❀

Kind and friendly gestures may encourage happy smiles
while understanding ears can be heard across the miles;
a shoulder loaned for leaning and hugs with good intent
are often tiny triggers enabling us to vent.

❀

Triumphant are the treasures trickling into our day,
moments making memories a welcoming display
of riches adding value to life's amazing ride,
representing happiness we love to store inside.

conquer

challenge

blossom

A Nudge is Often Needed

A nudge is often needed
to guide us into gear
by stimulating systems
held back through angst or fear.

❀

When vision's veiled by shadows,
it clouds our concrete goal
and tampers with our timing
to let our journey roll.

❀

An idle mind can stagnate,
suppress a simple thought
that otherwise could blossom
in preference to abort.

❀

Achievements often challenge
our deep and driving force,
rewarding us time over
for steering straight on course.

❀

Why not greet gracious nudges
to get ourselves in gear-
the gains are ours to cherish,
to conquer goals and cheer.

journey's

seeking

accepting

Mystery and Intrigue

Mystery and intrigue and challenge changing pace,
life's journey's our adventure running in the race,
rolling like a rubber ball bouncing to a beat,
striving to stay steadfast and balanced on our feet.

❧

Times can take our vision to summits soaring high,
sending spirits surging on sails across the sky,
beckoning forth beauty that beams in rainbow's hue,
showering us with sunshine's pleasures we pursue.

❧

Rugged roads rekindle the hardships up ahead,
gearing us through gateways, atremble as we tread,
fostering the feelings so often fed by fear,
manifesting raindrops that trickle like a tear.

❧

Mystery and intrigue and challenge changing pace,
attitude attributes to how we run the race—
seeking out the sunshine, accepting raindrops too,
breathing in the beauty bestowed in all we do.

Observing Humans

Observing humans is quite a game
always unique and never the same;

some common traits tend to trickle through-
watch family groups and things they do.

❋

Look at the gaits of father and son
as they stride in time like they are one.

Mimicking starts at an early age
so role model well at every stage.

❋

Check out the folk in a lengthy queue
and view body language leaking through-

sit in a bus on a bumpy ride
and see expressions some try to hide.

❋

Human behaviour portrays a tale
whether we're strong, bold, timid or frail;

even before we utter a sound
we set an image for all around.

❋

Judge not before we're given a chance
to truly know how others may dance.

family

image

unique

sharing

passage

enjoyment

On A Parallel Page

Disregard barriers of differing age
when minds are focused on a parallel page,
individuals sharing a common ground
connecting concurrently, actively bound.

❋

Behold the bondage that builds up between friends
who entertain interests of tangible trends,
travelling together through a passage of time,
rocking-n-rolling as their energies climb.

❋

Join in the journey where comradery rules,
fuelled by the feeling that is one of life's tools,
which saturates souls in insatiable ways,
enticing enjoyment through all of our days.

input

awakening

wisdom

Bundling Up Burdens

Bundling up burdens that weigh us down,
bombarding our brains and causing a frown,
hold purpose and meaning when they're let go,
allowing fresh input to ebb and flow.

❋

When a trusting ear and a caring soul
float into our orbit letting us roll
like free falling flowers drifting with ease,
the moment is ours to say as we please.

Sharing our sorrows, excitement and fears
release our emotions, laughter and tears,
awakening actions to gear ahead,
unleashing the chains once heavy as lead.

❋

Bundle those burdens and let them pass by,
shedding the shield that allows us to fly
with wings of wisdom from lessons we learn-
there's something to gain round every new turn.

optimism

wonderment

contentment

ENTHUSIASTIC ENERGY

Enthusiastic energy echoes far and wide,
enticing and empowering all within its stride
and bubbling like a fountain that flourishes and flows,
filters through the atmosphere as optimism grows.

❋

Boosted by a passion for fulfilling life with fun,
radiates remarkably like sunshine on the run,
gregariously greeting all those who wish to play,
continuously coaxing in an appealing way.

❋

Jump aboard the journey and join in the jolly game,
sharing the excitement is not really quite the same
as watching from the side-lines while others sing the song-
enthusiasm growing when 'goers' groove along.

❋

Enthusiastic energy echoes far and wide,
washes all with wonderment who wish to take the ride,
bubbling like a fountain with an effervescent flow,
filling all with freshness as contentment starts to grow.

relax

control

master

Rush Of Nerves

Riveted by a rush of nerves,
those would be smiles can change their curves,
adrenal glands pump over-time
as tension's tug begins to climb.

❀

Within, the mind is calling out-
'relax a while', we hear it shout,
yet captured in chaotic hue
the body blocks that basal cue.

❀

Unwanted waves of silent stress
challenge the feelings we address
and once the pressure passes by,
relief rewards us with a sigh.

❀

Control the notions nerves may cause,
with added breath and timely pause
and maybe when we least expect,
we'll master means that take effect.

wander

marvel

embrace

22

CLOSE YOUR EYES

Close your eyes and wander
where'er your mind may go
and let it set the pace
by following the flow.

❈

Aware of every sound
that echoes past your ears
relax into each breath
and filter out your fears.

❈

Float like a fleecy cloud
adrift a gentle breeze,
allowing limbs to lounge
like graceful arching trees.

❈

Sink into soul's embrace
and linger with the tide-
marvel in the moment
of life's refreshing ride.

lessons

gracious

thoughtfulness

To Give

To give's a gracious gesture,
a gift born from heart's desire
and comes with no attachments
when events as such transpire.

✻

On occasions we may find
there is reason to say no
and although we feel forlorn
we must let emotions go.

✻

Life's lessons are important
for our growth to gear ahead
and the art of consequence
is a path down which we're led.

✻

To give's a gracious gesture
and receiving's rather grand—
may thoughtfulness and wisdom
lead us sagely by the hand.

search

fantasies

refrain

Ridiculous Rumours

When ridiculous rumours rattle the brain
and their validity seems rather insane,
would we set them aside feeling quite forlorn
or search for the sources from which they were born?

❀

We may choose to laugh and allow them to fly
into the distance with the blink of an eye
and consciously cool about letting them go,
continue our course with unfaltering flow.

❀

Whatever reaction exists at the time
the spreading of rumours is really a crime,
as fictitious fantasies and facts confused
will travel in circles where few are amused.

❀

Well-meaning reminds us that we must refrain
from jumping on board that ridiculous train,
for rumours are remnants that shouldn't commence
and stories that spread at another's expense.

STEADILY STRIVING

Motivation may urge us along
sending us signals to sing our song,
steadily striving from strength to strength,
hopping through hurdles at any length.

❀

With self discipline, we strive alone
pushing ourselves as each seed is sown,
thinking beyond the finishing line,
resolving reason not to decline;

or leading sources select the pace
boosting morale to master the race,
gingerly gearing with driving praise,
powering us on in positive ways.

❀

Motivation's a marvellous tool-
how it's attained has no rigid rule;
work with it wisely in all we do-
it's a helping hand our whole life through.

discipline

strive

motivation

empathy

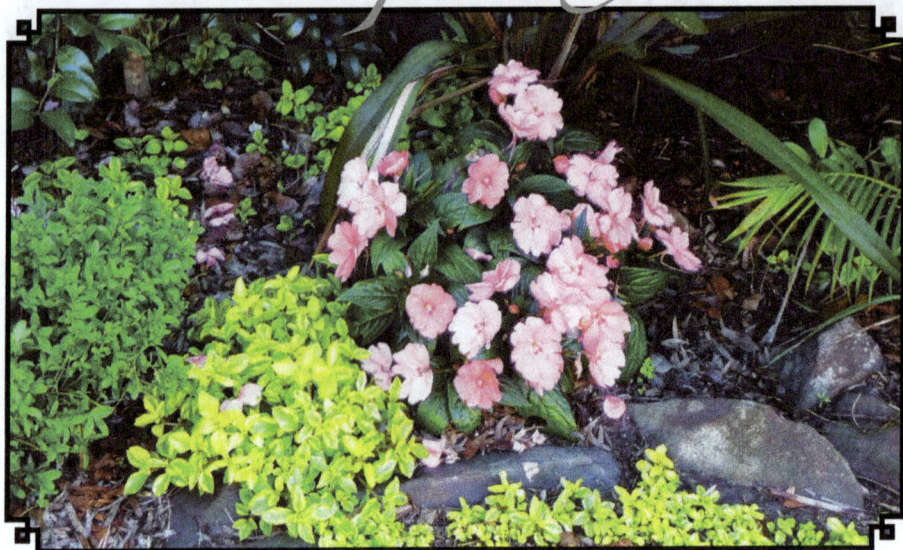

goodness

assuring

Gifts Of Goodness

Echoes of a listening ear
find fragments of a falling tear
and shelter it from stormy seas
with empathy to soothe and ease.

❧

A shoulder's strength to share the tale
of one whose heart is hit with hail
may be the base and stepping stone,
assuring that we're not alone.

❧

A helping hand and moment's grace
place smiles upon a fragile face,
when bubbles burst without control
and hearts reach out to heal a soul.

❧

Let's share the warmth we hold inside
with all who walk life's winding ride-
when gifts of goodness go around
they help to make our world profound.

Cherish The Love

Cherish the love like the flowers in spring,
that comes from a child and makes your heart sing,
sparkling your soul with a bubbling bouquet
of beautiful smiles that brighten your day.

❀

Listen to laughter that lights a child's face,
gregarious giggles gathering grace,
as beaming expressions dance in their eyes,
melting your mind like a magical prize.

❀

Frolic with freedom, enjoying child's play,
engage in their innocence on the way,
bouncing with energy, bounding along,
tirelessly tuned into life's happy song.

❀

Treasure the love of a child deep inside,
share the fulfilment that flavours the ride,
value its essence as journeys slip past
for the warmth felt within is made to last.

beautiful

magical

fulfilment

33

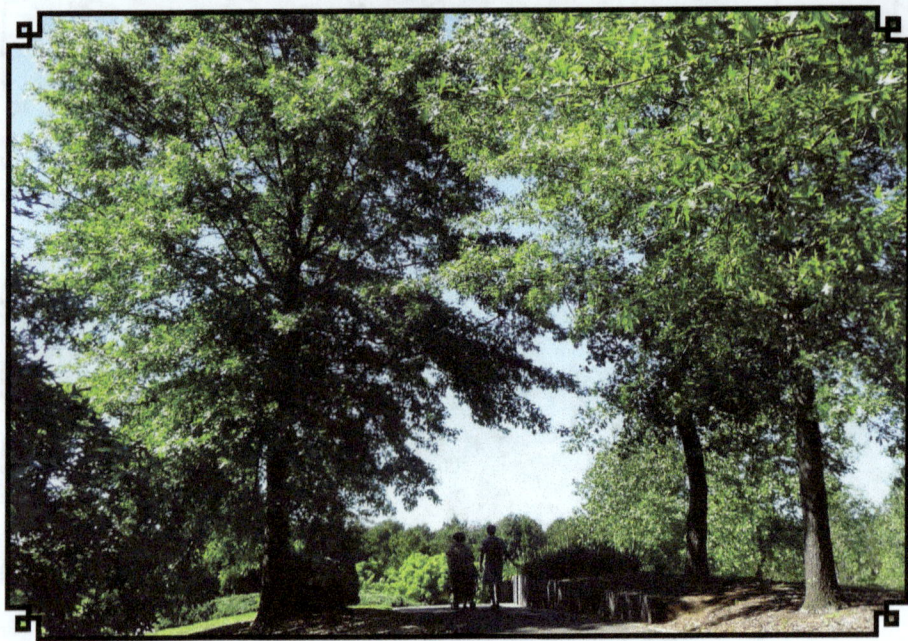

people

souls

encounter

PATHWAYS

Some breezes blow briskly passing through night,
telling their tales as the dark fades to light,

while whistling winds whirl and whisper in trees,
bringing refreshment and aiming to please

on warm sultry days when temperatures soar,
cooling and comforting all on earth's floor;

perhaps with purpose and meaning for all
existing today on life's roller-ball.

❋

Such is the pathway of people we meet-
some souls slide silently after we greet,

while others lovingly linger along,
finding room in our hearts where they belong;

each with purpose as our journey rolls past,
every encounter is carefully cast,

guiding us forward on destiny's way,
planting fresh seeds to be nurtured each day.

hopes

dreams

light

LIGHT THE FIRE IN LIFE

Light the fire in life wherever we are
and keep it aglow as our journey spreads far,
for whatever our purpose, our hopes or dreams,
we should kindle the flame, for that's how it seems.

❀

Linger not on regrets nor dwell on the past.
Look to the future and the joys it may cast,
for we cannot retrieve what has sailed on by,
though we can move ahead if we choose to try.

❀

Over mountains we climb and valleys we stride,
along each terrain there's a reason we ride,
forever striving to maintain happiness
as time passes by and our journeys progress.

❀

Keep the spark in life's pathway alive and bright
and hang onto its warmth as day turns to night,
for this journey is ours, allow it to flow,
feeling love in our hearts wherever we go.

enjoy

unwind

laugh

REVEL IN FUN

Let loose and feel excitement grow,
remove the mask that hides our glow,
feel all our inhibitions slide,
adventure forth enjoy the ride.

❦

Take off the back-pack full of woes
and feel the weight lift from our toes,
ready to dance with fleeting grace
as beaming smiles adorn the face.

❦

Responsibilities shall be
a part of life for you and me,
but never lose that spark we own
where having fun is overgrown.

❦

Let loose, enjoy with all our might,
unwind and laugh if we're uptight,
relax and let our sparkle show-
and revel in the fun-filled flow.

Power Of Persuasion

Power of persuasion is a force all its own,
often delivered where uncertainty's sown
and when edged with enthusiastic appeal
is the energy needed to seal a deal.

❀

It filters through varying facets of life
by serving us well or attuning to strife,
frequently focuses on changing the mind
viewing perspectives of a differing kind.

❀

When persuasive powers are swinging our way
consider the options which come into play,
by taking the time to let thoughts trickle past,
investing in interests both wise and steadfast.

❀

Allow intuition to guide us along,
making decisions is our personal song-
the power of persuasion's a reckoning force-
let's trust in ourselves as we take the right course.

persuasion

options

trust

live

love

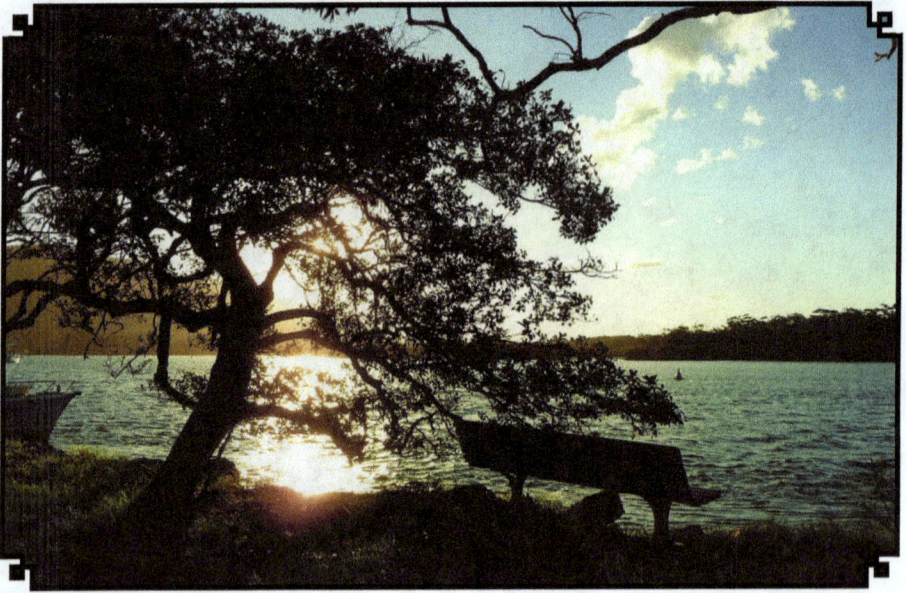

peace

NESTLED

Nestled beneath beautiful branching bowers,
sun-rays are beaming like silvery showers,
glistening and gliding on the glassy lake
as pelicans pause for a splash and a shake.

❀

The silence is broken by beckoning birds,
the voice of wind whispering whistling words,
while it loiters through leaves as they swish and sway
on this first day of Spring, while time drifts away.

❀

Such peaceful surrounds soothe and mellow the mind
and the pace of the week is long left behind,
as leisure-time luxury allows for rest,
absorbing the tranquil terrain at its best.

❀

Live life to the fullest with laughter and love,
respectful of earth and the Heavens above-
share amongst others as we give with our hearts,
knowing peace from within is where it all starts.

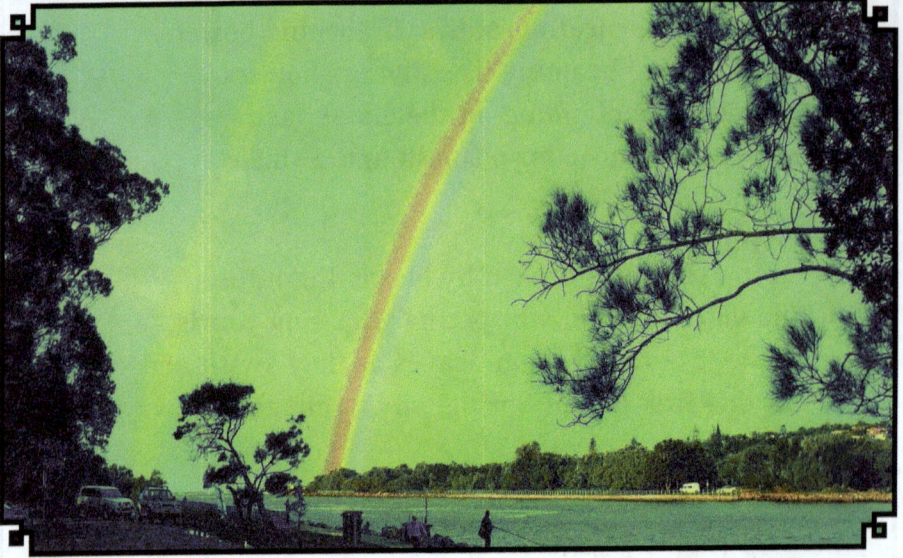

visualize

seek

explore

44

Look Beyond The Finish Line

Look beyond the finish line
where fresh beginnings rise,
and visualize the future
that's filled with new surprise.

❀

Whatever past was made of,
we choose the road ahead
if the knowledge gained before
plants wisdom in our head.

❀

Opportunities await
behind the opaque door,
and if we venture through it
the world's ours to explore.

❀

Forever seek the sunshine
that brightens each new day,
and dance upon life's rainbows
in colourful array.

emotions

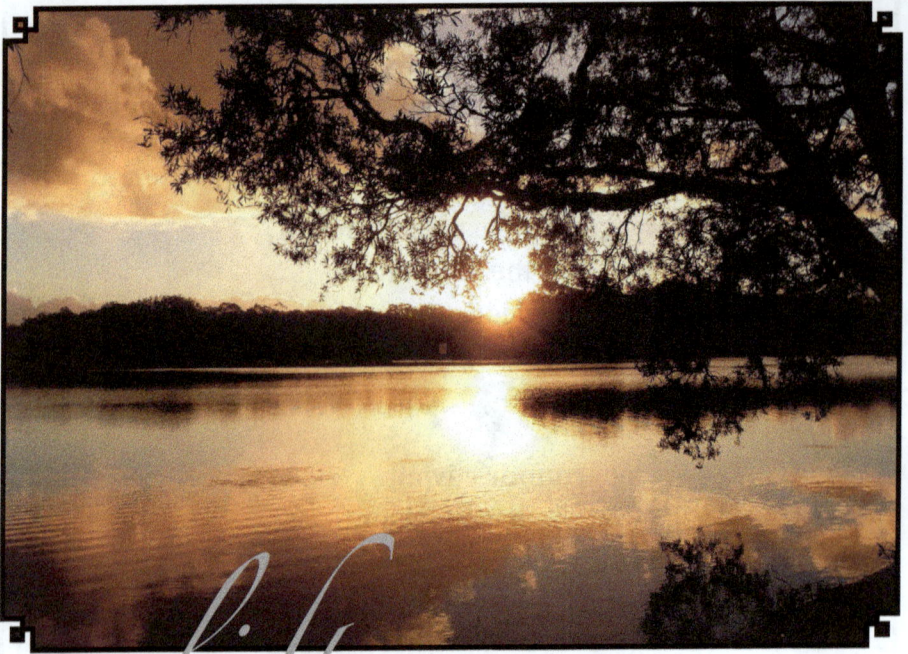

lift

surprise

LIFT OUR SPIRITS

Moments which lift our spirits
may come from near or far
and trigger our emotions
like sparkles in a star.

❊

Come in many different ways
and tap into our soul,
warming presence from within
that takes us on a roll-

riding high on outspread wings,
where happiness resides
and pleasing thoughts surround us
as time just slips and slides.

❊

When e'er our spirit's rising,
enjoy and let it flow,
it's one of life's surprises
that sets our world aglow.

Release Your Inner Child

Release your inner child within,
let inhibitions slide
and feel the joy in letting go
of thoughts you often hide.

❀

Allow yourself to laugh out loud;
it truly does you good;
and don't bottle up emotions
because you think you should.

❀

Remember child-like playfulness,
pure innocence and glee,
all the fun-filled games and laughter
that let your heart run free.

❀

It's tucked inside our adulthood,
awaiting a release
and laughing without a reason
helps strengthen inner peace.

❀

Please have a go and laugh out loud-
see how it makes you feel;
the benefits you have to gain
are absolutely real.

innocence

playfulness

glee

love

strength

greatness

Allow Love In

Allow love in and feel its glow,
hold it close and let it grow
like sunshine in a summer sky,
bringing sparkles to our eye.

❀

Find love in the simplest things,
gentle breeze, a bird that sings,
a friendly smile, a calming voice;
look about there's so much choice.

❀

Wear love always inside our heart,
ours to keep right from the start,
and let it not drift far away,
love to live throughout each day.

❀

Love brings strength to linger longer,
warms our soul, makes us stronger;
allow love in and feel its glow,
greatest joy we'll ever know.

ride

learn

gain

Life's Bicycle

Life's journey's ever changing
as our circumstances roll,
presenting new adventures
whilst we challenge every goal.

❀

Some are set to test our skills
and detect how well we cope,
urging us to surge ahead
with encouragement and hope.

❀

Others flow like silent streams
as calm waters amble past,
moments of tranquillity
when our peaceful thoughts are cast.

❀

In between we bounce along
balancing the highs and lows,
like triggers in our journey
which shall keep us on our toes.

❀

Jump upon life's bicycle
and ride with respect and care,
lots to learn and much to gain
anytime and anywhere.

live

life

free

Share Your Life With Laughter

Share your life with laughter
and love to live each day,
our future is unknown,
today is ours to play.

❈

Express love for others
and let your feelings show,
hide not your warmest thoughts,
emotions need to flow.

❈

Daring to be different,
a privilege all our own;
spontaneous events
may help fresh seeds be sown.

❈

Keep hope within your heart
and reach out for your dreams,
conscious that each journey's
not always as it seems.

❈

No time like the present,
be who you want to be,
it's how we feel inside
that truly sets us free.

forgiveness

courage

understanding

Waste Not Good Energy

Waste not good energy
by harbouring a grudge,
for no purpose is gained
when resisting to budge.

❧

Those pent up emotions
bring us negative stress,
and play on health issues
until time of address.

❧

Forgiveness takes courage
bringing freedom of mind,
while dealing with the truth
helps our thoughts to unwind.

❧

And when energy burned
is a positive force,
we overcome the angst
in life's obstacle course.

❧

Time and understanding
help us heal from inside-
releasing our grudges
shall bring peace to our ride.

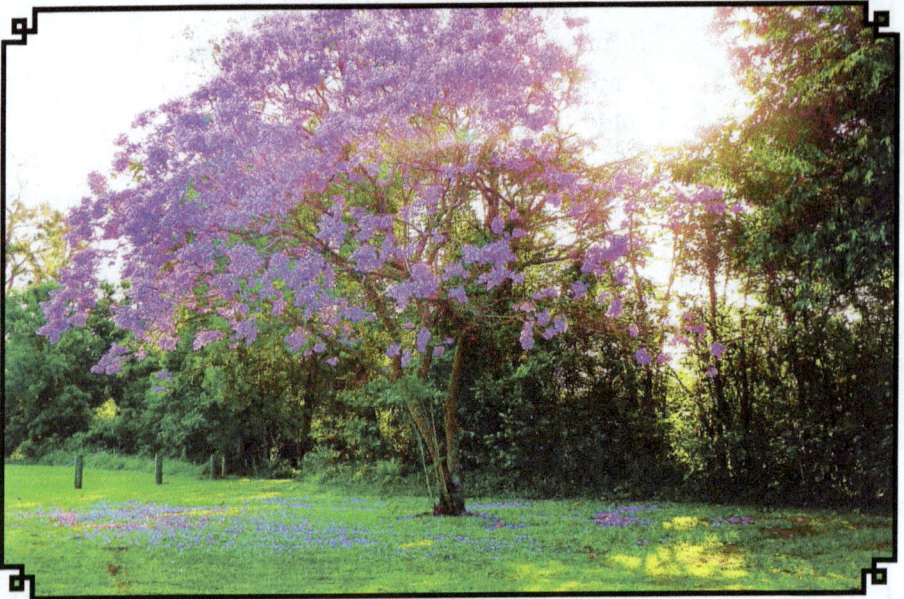

listening

wisdom

care

Elderly Folk

Elderly folk have so much to share,
if only the world was more aware
of all the wisdom they store inside,
and the joy of joining in their ride.

❀

With listening ears to sit awhile,
a friendly chat and a sincere smile,
you can feel their spirit start to glow-
a welcome change from their TV show.

❀

Exchanging thoughts and personal views
drive conversations, provide new cues,
keep discussions on a winning role-
happiness being the greatest goal.

❀

Elderly folk - we shall all grow there!
May our journeys flow with love and care;
set aside some time as life spins past,
moments we share are memories that last.

open

mind

clarity

When Thoughts Spin Round

When thoughts spin round and round again
and answers aren't quite clear,
no need for jumping up and down
until the pathway's clear.

❀

Sometimes we need a little space
to sort and correlate,
allow the mind to chill awhile
when excess fills our plate.

❀

Step aside where the air is fresh
and let the tension go,
inhale the new with open mind
and feel the goodness flow.

❀

Close the eyes while imagining
warm sunshine up above,
surround yourself with happy thoughts
that shower you with love.

❀

And when the time is right for you
clarity shall return,
as thoughts and feelings unresolved
find answers that you yearn.

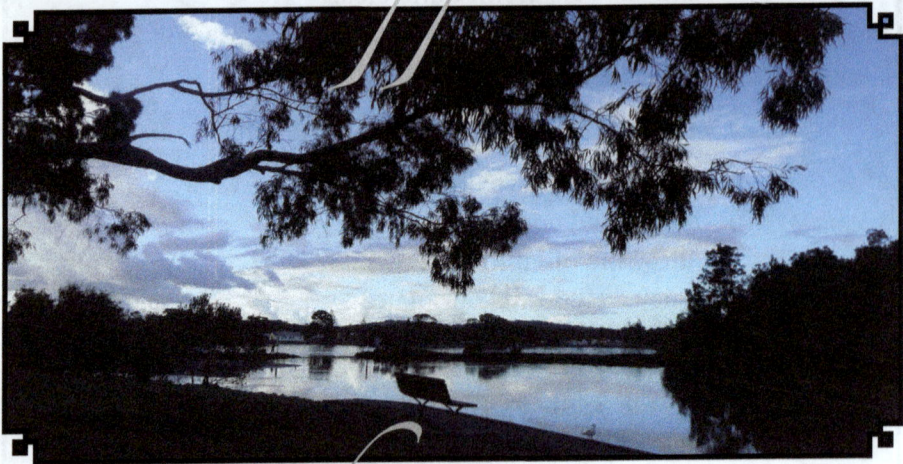

approach

speak

care

Airing Thoughts

Airing thoughts and feelings within,
is a wise approach, not a sin,
if words are chosen using tact
to draw attention to the fact.

❧

Too easily wrong words slip out,
fill the listener's mind with doubt,
as offence lingers in their head,
misguided by what has been said.

❧

Taking a breath before we speak,
can save us having tongue in cheek;
a little pause gives time to think-
less chance of falling in the brink.

❧

Whenever we have thoughts to air,
let's choose our words with lots of care;
truths may be shared on any day
if tact is used in all we say.

time

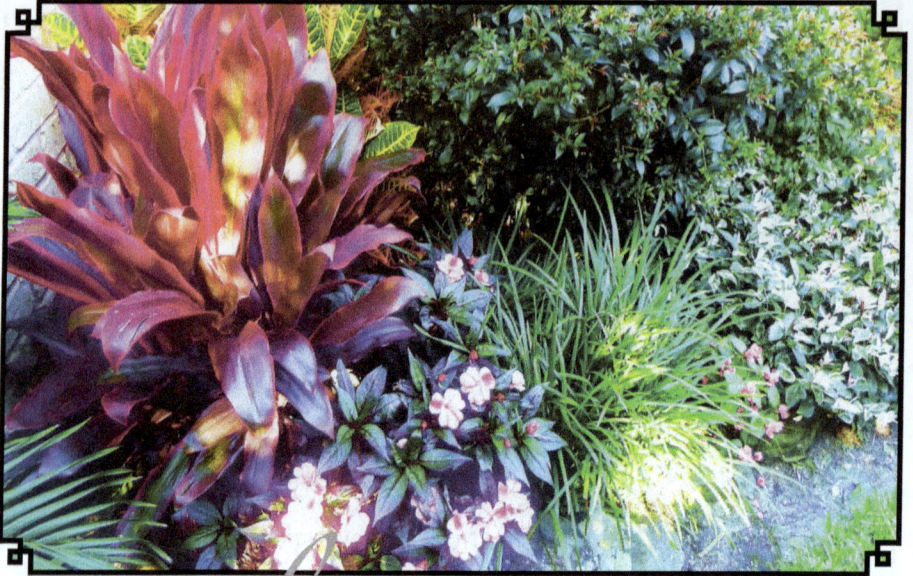

place

awareness

Life's Little Messengers

Life's little messengers are all around,
if we open our eyes they can be found;
not always subtle, nor matter of fact,
and often relate to how we react.

❀

Chance meetings that occur right time and place,
a welcoming smile on a passing face,
kind words delivered that touch heart and soul,
and gestures that help us attain a goal.

❀

If there is reason in all we pursue,
we should practice patience in all things new,
listen to words that offer us advice,
make no assumptions before thinking twice.

❀

Life's little messengers are ours to find,
drawing self-awareness into the mind,
opening our eyes as our journeys roll,
and helping us to focus on each new goal.

REAL FRIENDS ROCK

No strings are attached
both trusting and true
loyal and caring
reliable too

        Real friends rock

Lend us a shoulder
a listening ear
share in our laughter
and wipe up a tear

        Real friends rock

Offer us guidance
when times become rough
and see through our mask
though we're acting tough

        Real friends rock

True friends are treasures
family we choose
sharing a friendship
through good times and blues

❆

So blessed is a soul
to have a real friend
cherish the feeling
until journey's end

❆

        Real friends rock

cherish

reliable

treasures

thoughtfulness

refreshing

gifts

Thoughtful Gestures

Thoughtful gestures can make our day,
grown from the heart, given away;
no strings attached for their reclaim,
born out of love from whence they came.

❀

Don't overlook the little things,
the source from where much pleasure springs,
which lift the mood and bring a smile
and make the moment so worthwhile.

❀

A simple touch of thoughtfulness
is something we may all address,
and in a kind refreshing way
these precious gifts shall light our day.

❀

Give a thought and receive with pride,
both gestures make an awesome ride,
as sunshine coming from the heart
shall give each day a fresh new start.

loving

memories

special

REMINISCING

Reminiscing over years gone by
as photos are flashing past the eye;
memories turning on emotion,
washing the soul with sweet devotion.

Happy moments that last forever,
stored inside for the heart to treasure,
and again recaptured on demand,
as long passed images come to hand.

A son, a daughter, so young and free,
celebrating their life filled with glee,
living the journey of childlike play
until adulthood comes by one day.

❅

As years wash by like an ocean wave,
those loving memories are ours to save,
and now our sons and our daughters too,
are parents with kids, like me and you.

We look at the pictures and compare
familiar features and baby hair,
the beautiful grandkids we admire,
and the way they set our hearts on fire.

Nothing equals the love of our child,
whether they're good or a little wild;
grandkids too, bring the same special love-
a joy to share till we fly above.

enthusiasm

triumphantly

rewarding

Some Missions Seem Impossible

Some missions seem impossible,
too much to take on board,
yet intuition beckons us-
go forth and seek reward.

❊

Breaking down all the barriers,
which block the starting line,
unleash initial progress,
at times, hard to define.

Prompts from others may often help
to boost our confidence,
encourage us with little steps,
so tasks don't seem immense.

❊

When enthusiasm drives us,
there is no holding back;
we surge ahead triumphantly
along our winning track,

and regardless of the outcome,
our will to have a go,
must be the most rewarding seed
that we could wish to sow.

establish

new
gateways

Baggage

Baggage is so often stored away,
inner emotions from yesterday;
weighs more and more as the time goes by,
reflected within the owner's eye.

❀

Manifests itself in many ways,
through outbursts of indirect displays,
of pain and anger, mistrust and fears,
producing sadness and stress and tears.

❀

Dealing with all our issues and strains,
shall help us establish future gains,
as gateways, once under lock and key,
gradually open as thoughts run free.

❀

Time and management lessen the load,
no longer travelling one way road;
dust and debris being left behind,
clearing the path, with no axe to grind.

❀

Excess baggage never needs a home,
wave it good bye, allow it to roam,
to yonder pastures, beyond the view,
make room for journeys, afresh and new.

creation

beauty

quality

$\mathcal{B}$IGGEST $\mathcal{I}$SN'T $\mathcal{A}$LWAYS $\mathcal{B}$EST

$\mathcal{B}$iggest isn't always best,
life's joys aren't measured by size,
like the bonsai, so minute,
it's within, where beauty lies.

$\mathcal{B}$roadest panoramic views
may dazzle the eyes in awe,
yet splendour of creation
permeates from inner core.

$\mathcal{A}$ feast is only as large
as expectations demand,
grandiose or miniscule,
dependant on mind's command.

❦

$\mathcal{B}$ig
little
matters not
inner beauty
shall conquer the heart
two words may say as much
as one thousand lines impart

and guided by the essence
for true strength dwells inside
judge not quantity
for quality
shall fulfil
every
ride

77

About the Author

Mel Stewart finds her inspiration from life's colourful journey and is especially drawn to nature where she puts pen to paper to express her emotions about everyday occurrences. Living on the mid north coast of N.S.W. Australia provides an abundance of natural water resources for Mel to further her creativity in photography.

She enjoys sharing her own thoughts and feelings about love and laughter, and the ups and downs that confront us on a daily basis, maintaining a positive outlook and her choice to find happiness in the simplest of things.

Follow Mel Stewart on Facebook @ Mel's Art
Website   www.mels-art.com.au